NATIONAL GEOGRAPHIC

T0045265

Numbers in Our World

Rachel Griffiths and
Margaret Clyne

OLD TOWN

We see numbers on the clock.

What do the numbers tell us?

8
MPH

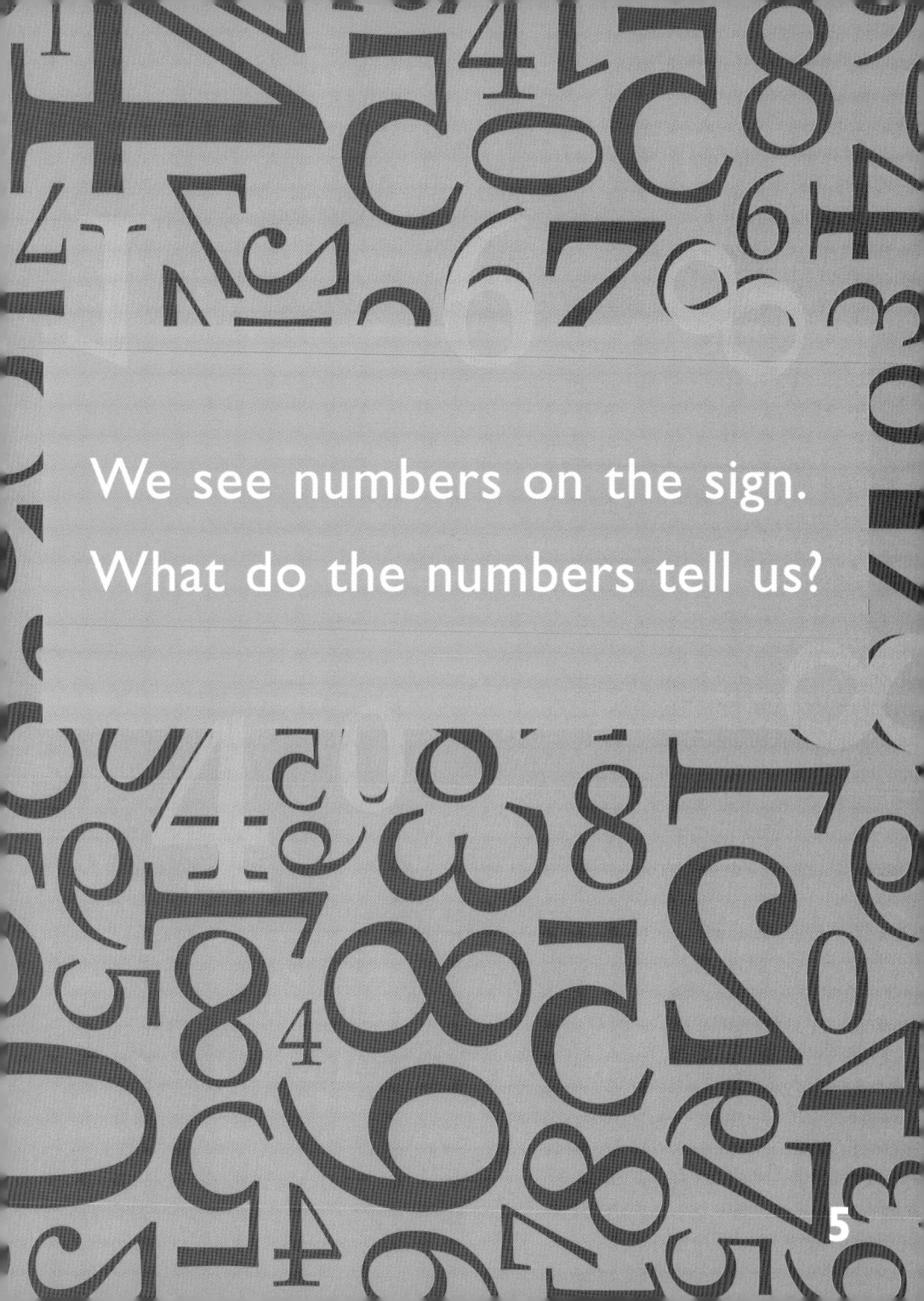

We see numbers on the sign.

What do the numbers tell us?

44

We see numbers on the door.

What do the numbers tell us?

FALCON
23
23
23

We see numbers on the shirts.

What do the numbers tell us?

3
4
HENRY
BUTTERWORTH
5
10
ROULE
LAMARCHE
11
12

We see numbers on
the mailboxes.
What do the numbers tell us?

We see numbers at the market.
What do the numbers tell us?